THE
HOLY LAND

Photography: Garo Nalbandian

Palphot

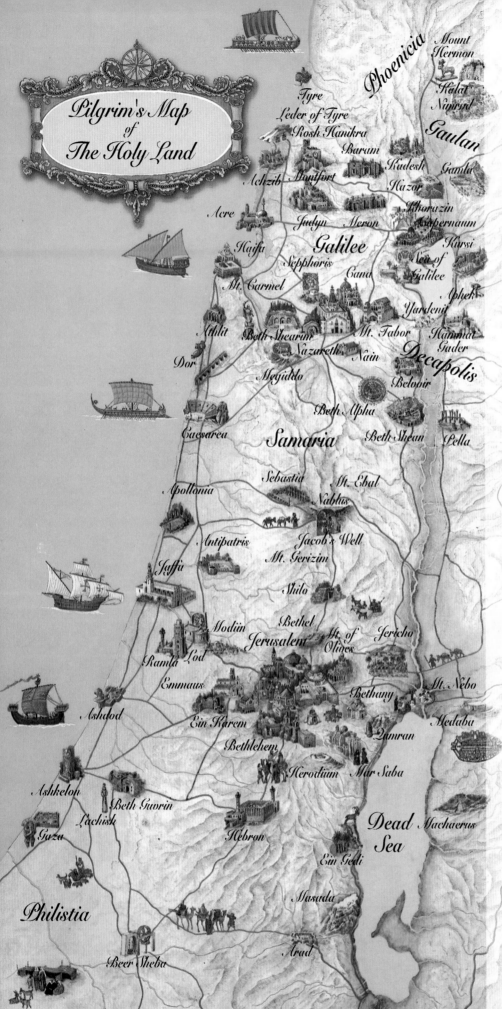

Pilgrim's Map of The Holy Land

Contents

Introduction 3
Nazareth 4-7
Ein Karem 8-10
Bethlehem 11-25
Herodion 26
St Mary & Solomon's Pools 27
Nazareth 28-31
Sepphoris 32
Cana 33-34
Mount Tabor 35-40
Capernaum 41-43
Tabgha 44-45
Dalmanutha 46
St Peter's Primacy 47-48
Mount of Beatitudes 49-51
Korazin, Kursi 52-53
Caesarea Philippi, Yardenit 54-55
Mount Gilboa 56-57
Mount of Temptation 58
Jericho 59-60
Qumran 61-62
Ein Gedi 63
Dead Sea 64
Masada 65
Jerusalem 66-67
Bethany 68-69
Bethphage 70
Pater Noster 71
Mount of Olives .72-73
Dome of Ascension 74
City of David 75
Hagia Maria Zion 76-77
Coenaculum 78
Kidron Valley 79
Dominus Flevit 80
Gethsemane 81
Basilica of Agony .82
Tomb of Virgin Mary 83
Russian Church 84
Pool of Siloam 85
St. Peter in Gallicantu 86-87
Pools of Bethesda .88
Church of St. Anne 89
Via Dolorosa 92-98
Church of the Holy Sepulcher 99-107
Different Christian sects 108-109
Garden Tomb 111
Emmaus 112-113
Dome of the Rock 114-116
Mosque of El Aksa 117
Golden Gate 118
Damascus Gate 119
Gates of Jerusalem 120-121
Tower of David 122
Western Wall tunnels 123
Western Wall .124-125
Shrine of the Book 126
Holyland Model 127
Bedouin 128
Hebron 129
Megiddo, Samaria 130
Bet Shean 131
Tiberias 132
Mount Arbel 133
Hula Valley, Mt. Hermon 134
Acre 135
Haifa 136
Stella Maris 137
Caesarea 138
Jaffa 139
Ashdod, Ashkelon 140
Beersheba 141
Nabateans 142
Eilat 143
Medaba map 144

© Copyright Palphot Ltd. - P.O. Box 2 - Herzlia - Israel

All rights reserved. No part of this publication may be reproduced in any form or by any means without the prior permission of the copyright owner.

Prepared with the assistance of the Studium Biblicum Franciscanum

Printed in Israel.

Photographers: Garo Nalbandian
Aerial photographs: Duby Tal and Moni Haramati

ISBN 965-280-125-9

Introduction

Two millennia have passed since the Annunciation to Mary of Nazareth, the event that marks the start of the Christian era.

For two thousand years, a constant flow of pilgrims has been coming to the Holy Land to visit the sacred places where the Gospel was preached. They come to the city of Jerusalem which, St. Paul writes, will be the center of the New Order.

In the sixth century, an artist created a mosaic map marking sites mentioned in the Bible. This map, which is in Madaba in Jordan, shows the area of the Holy Land, Jordan, Lebanon, Syria and the Sinai desert and Nile Delta in Egypt. The Near East becomes an enlarged Holy Land, reaching its figurative peak in the depiction of Jerusalem, which is given clear theological significance as the center of the world. The Near East without borders becomes the symbol of a new reality of peace.

A pilgrimage is the best way to discover the Holy Land and understand the Gospels, reading passages at the sacred sites connected with them. If you have had the privilege of visiting the Land, this book can help you relive these wonderful days. However, those not able to visit the Land in which Jesus chose to be born and live His life can get to know it through the magnificent pictures and descriptions in this book.

May this book bring much joy and understanding to many people.

Fr. Benedikt

The Basilica
of the
Annunciation
Nazareth

The city of Nazareth lies in a valley in the southern Galilee. Here the Angel Gabriel announced to the Virgin Mary that she would bear a child, and here Jesus spent his childhood with his parents Joseph and Mary: *"And he came and dwelt in a city called Nazareth: that it might be fulfilled which was spoken by the prophets, he shall be called a Nazarene"* (Matthew 2:23).

In the first centuries A.D., Nazareth was populated only by Jews, but with the strengthening of the Roman Empire, the number of Christians living there grew. From the fourth century onwards, churches were built on the sites that were connected with Jesus and the Virgin Mary.

Today the population of Nazareth comprises Christians, Moslems and Jews. The Christians belong to various denominations: Roman Catholic, Greek Catholic, Greek Orthodox, Maronite, Anglican, Copt, Armenian, Baptist and other Protestant sects. There are many churches, monasteries and convents, hostels, hospitals and schools maintained by various denominations.

The Basilica of the Annunciation, built on the spot where Gabriel appeared to Mary, was completed in 1969 and dominates the city. It is the fifth church built on the spot where the Angel Gabriel stood when he prophesied to the Virgin Mary that she would conceive a child, and remains of the earlier churches can still be seen.

The Grotto, the holiest area in the Basilica of the Annunciation

The Crypt in the Basilica of the Annunciation

Torso of a statue of St. Peter holding the church and the key to the "Kingdom of Heaven".

← Detail of the Zodiac

Cave-dwelling in the village (Cave of the capitals)

Medieval or Romanesque capitals from the Crusaders' Church.

..."The angel Gabriel was sent from God unto a city of Galilee named Nazareth.... And the angel ...said unto her, Fear not Mary: for thou hast found favour with God. And, behold, thou shalt conceive in thy womb, and bring forth a son, and shalt call his name Jesus."

Luke 1:26-31

EIN KAREM

" A nd Mary arose in those days, and went into the hill country with haste into a city of Judah, and entered into the house of Zacharias, and saluted Elisabeth" (Luke 1:39-40).

According to tradition, Ein Karem is the "city of Judah" associated with the life of John the Baptist. Here Zacharias, John the Baptist's father, had his summer home, and here the Virgin Mary visited her cousin Elizabeth. Churches, convents and monasteries abound in the picturesque valley. The seventeenth century Church of St. John the Baptist was built over the birthplace of St. John. The first church on the site was built under the Byzantines and rebuilt by the Crusaders, but later destroyed. It has beautiful paintings

The Church of the Visitation
Interior of the Church of the Visitation

Interior of the Church of the Visitation

and decorated ceramic tiles. Steps lead down to a natural cave, the Grotto of the Birth of St. John. On the lintel is inscribed a verse from the 'Benedictus': "Blessed be the Lord, God of Israel; for he hath visited and redeemed his people". The architect Barluzzi designed the Church of the Visitation on the site of the home of Elizabeth and Zacharias. It was built in 1935 over the remains of former churches, the first from the fourth century. Inside the Church is a fresco depicting the visit of the Virgin Mary and below are the altar and ancient well. In the crypt of the Church there is a rock where, traditionally, the Infant John was concealed during the Massacre of the Innocents.

Sanctuary of the Visitation - The Magnificat

General view of Ein Karem

The Baptism
of Jesus
by St. John,
Ein Karem

Left:
The Grotto of the Benedictus,
under whose altar is a star marking
the place where John the Baptist was born.

Below:
The Church of St. John the Baptist
in the center of Ein Karem.
The first church was built in the fifth century A.D.
A beautiful mosaic floor from that period has survived,
depicting peacocks, birds and flowers.

BETHLEHEM

Fresco depicting
the angel announcing
the birth of Jesus
to the shepherds.

The Holy Family

Interior of the Shepherds' Field Church

Grotto of the Shepherds' Field Church

Bethlehem, which in Hebrew means "house of bread", was originally called Ephrath, and has many biblical associations reflecting a tranquil, pastoral existence. Here Jacob buried his beloved wife Rachel (Gen.35:16) and here was enacted the story of Ruth. Bethlehem is revered as the birthplace of David (I Sam. 17:12) and of Jesus, *"born in Bethlehem of Judaea in the days of Herod the King"* (Mat. 2:1).

East of Bethlehem, in the village of Beit Sahur, is the Shepherds' Field where the Angel appeared to the shepherds and announced the birth of Jesus: *"Fear not: for, behold, I bring you good tidings of great joy, which shall be to all people. For unto you is born this day in the City of David a Saviour, which is Christ the Lord"* (Luke 2:10-11). There is a Greek Orthodox Church built over a cave and another church was built for the Franciscans by Barluzzi in 1950.

The Shepherds' Field

The Shepherds' Field Church

Church of the Nativity with the Church of St. Catherine on the left

Wooden panel in the Basilica of the Nativity

Joseph and Mary came from Nazareth to Bethlehem for the census ordered by the Roman authorities because Joseph was of the lineage of David, and Bethlehem was the "city of David". The Gospel of Luke (2:7) describes how Mary *"brought forth her firstborn son... and laid him in a manger; because there was not room in the inn."* From the very beginnings of Christianity, the grotto where Jesus was born was sacred. The first church was built over the grotto

◄ ....

Overshadowed by the massive stone walls of the Basilica of the Nativity is the Door of Humility, the small doorway to the church.

Basilica of the Nativity, which has four rows of twelve brown Bethlehem stone pillars.

in the first half of the fourth century on the initiative of the Byzantine Emperor Constantine and his mother, the Empress Helena. The octagonal altar they erected is still there. This church was partially destroyed in the Samaritan revolt of the sixth century. The present church was built by Justinian in 530. From the exterior, it appears like a fortress. The original entrance was filled in and made low and narrow in order to protect it from the Moslem invaders and to prevent them from entering on horseback.

*Right:
Detail of
a column
in the Basilica
of the Nativity*

*Below:
A well-preserved
remnant of the
original mosaic
floor showing the
intricate geometric
design and subtle
colours used.*

*Mosaic representation of the Regional Council
held at Antioch, from the wall decoration
in the Basilica of the Nativity.*

Entrance to the Grotto of the Nativity.
Armenian Christians at prayer in front of the Nativity Altar.
On the right, Altar of the Magi (the Three Kings).

Procession to the Grotto of the Nativity
on Christmas Eve with the Latin patriarch of Jerusalem.

Most churches in the Holy Land were destroyed during the Persian invasion of the seventh century, but apparently the Church of the Nativity was saved from desecration because of the mosaic then on the facade of the Church, which depicted the Three Wise Men who came to pay homage to the baby Jesus (Matthew 2:2) in Persian clothing.

They restored the interior of the church, but its basic shape remained the same. The lower parts of the walls were covered with marble panels, while the upper part was decorated with mosaics. On the limestone columns were paintings of the Apostles. Over the years, the Crusader decorations were destroyed and today the two rows of red limestone columns stand starkly in the austere church beneath the oak ceiling that was presented by Edward IV of England and Philip Duke of Burgundy in 1482. Remains of the original mosaic floor from Helena's church can be seen through trapdoors in the floor.

Over the centuries the Church changed hands many times and today it is shared by the Greek Orthodox, the Latins and the Armenians.

The silver star in the Grotto of the Nativity.
This denotes the spot where Jesus was born.
The inscription reads:
Hic De Virgine Maria Jesus Christus Natus Est
Here Jesus Christ was born of the Virgin Mary.

*Crusader bishop's staff
from the twelfth century*

The Franciscan Church of St. Catherine of Alexandria was built in **1881** next to the Church of the Nativity, over the ruins of a twelfth century Crusader church. It was restored by Antonio Barluzzi in 1933. Inside the Church are the Chapel of St. Joseph and the Chapel of the Innocents and in front is a beautiful Crusader cloister. The Latin Patriarch officiates at Midnight Mass on Christmas Eve, which is attended by many pilgrims and broadcast all over the world.

December 24, the Christmas procession in Manger Square

Statue of St. Jerome in front of St. Catherine's Church. The death's head at the base of the monument symbolizes the saint's ascetic way of life and also human mortality.

The Church of St. Catherine on Christmas Eve Insert: The Patriarch carries the Child of Bethlehem

The Church of the Nativity on Christmas Eve

*Arabs riding their camels
in the vicinity of Bethlehem,
reminiscent of the "Three Wise Men"*

Nativity Seal

The Milk Grotto

The milky-white Church of the Milk Grotto is a Franciscan chapel built over the cave in which the Holy Family sheltered during the flight to Egypt. Tradition holds that a drop of milk that fell from Mary's breast while she was nursing Jesus caused the white color of the chalk in the Milk Grotto. New mothers collect the chalk and mix it with their food to ensure a plentiful supply of milk.

The entrance to the Franciscan church which was built in 1871 over the Milk Grotto.

Below:
The interior of the Milk Grotto which commemorates the Christian doctrine of the Divine Maternity of the Virgin Mary.

Ornament of a capital from the Milk Grotto in Bethlehem

The Tomb of Rachel

"And Rachel died, and was buried on the way to Ephrat, which is Bethlehem. And Jacob set a pillar upon her grave: That is the pillar of Rachel's grave unto this day."
(Genesis 35:19-20)

The Tomb of Rachel, a small domed structure, is venerated by Jews, Christians and Moslems. To this day Jews come to pray here in times of trouble, especially women who pray for fertility and safe childbirth.

Workers in a candle factory

Syrian Orthodox priest with Aramaic bible

Olivewood handicraft

At the market
in Bethlehem

The Market

On weekday mornings, Manger Square is alive with a typical Oriental market, attended by women from the surrounding villages wearing the traditional colorful local dress. Here one can find everything from sweet Arab cakes dripping in honey to statuettes and other artifacts carved in olivewood. Mother-of-pearl religious objects are also made here; in the late sixteenth century, the custodian of Bethlehem encouraged the poverty-stricken inhabitants to make these souvenirs for sale to the pilgrims. To this day, most Bethlehemites live off tourism and many are skilled artisans and craftsmen.

People of Bethlehem

Inserts on the opposite page:
Left: Bethlehem in Hebrew is "House of Bread"
Right: "Bethlehem" in Arabic is "House of Meat"

The Hill of Herodion

The fortress of Herod is located seven kilometres south-east of Bethlehem. Herodion, one of many fortresses built by Herod, was planned as a refuge from his many enemies in Jerusalem. Archaeological excavations have revealed remains of palaces, fortification towers, bath-houses, tremendous under-ground cisterns and an aqueduct bringing water from afar.

Before his death, Herod asked to be buried at Herodion and according to Josephus, he was indeed interred here.

St. Mary
of the Hortus Conclusus

St. Mary of the Hortus Conclusus is a convent that was built in the nineteenth century by an Argentinian bishop. The small fertile valley in which it is situated is said to be the enclosed garden, the hortus conclusus, of the Song of Solomon 4:12: *"A garden inclosed is my sister, my spouse"*.

St. Mary of the Hortus Conclusus

Solomon's Pools

Three huge triple reservoirs known as "Solomon's Pools" after the verse: *"I made me pools of water to irrigate a grove of growing trees"* (Ecclesiastes 2:6). The pools were constructed at the time of Herod to collect rainwater from the surrounding hills to supply Jerusalem with water all year round.

Sheep grazing near Bethlehem

Solomon's Pools

NAZARETH

The Holy Family

Partial view of Nazareth

The Church of St. Joseph

Joseph and his family *"returned into Galilee, to their own city Nazareth"* (Luke 2:39). Opposite the Church of the Annunciation is the Church of St. Joseph, built over the cave which served as Joseph's workshop. Another tradition holds that it was the home of the Holy Family. The present church was built over the remains of Byzantine and Crusader churches, which can still be seen in the crypt. Beneath the crypt is the Holy Cave and beside it, a water cistern.

◄ ....
Opposite: General view of Nazareth

The Grotto under the Church of St Joseph, with silos

The Holy Family

The Church
of St Joseph

Baptismal basin in the crypt of the Church of St Joseph

Interior of the
Church of St Joseph

Mary's Well

Church of St. Gabriel ················▶

Mary's Well in the Church of St. Gabriel

The Church of St. Gabriel

Mary's Well ·············▶

The present Greek Orthodox church was built over Mary's Well and is also known as the house of Mary. The church dates back to 1741 and was built on the site of Byzantine and Crusader churches.

St Anne's Church

Aramaic inscription from mosaic in synagogue at Sepphoris

Sepphoris

Sepphoris, or Zippori, near Nazareth, was the largest city in the Galilee at the time of Jesus, and was the home of Mary's parents, Anne and Joachim. Although it is not mentioned in the Bible, it is very likely that Jesus spent time here and that it served as the setting for some of his sermons mentioning the "big city". A 4000 seat amphitheater, streets, a water system, houses with magnificent mosaic floors and public buildings from the Roman and Byzantine periods have been unearthed and the remains of a Crusader fortress crowns the hill.

Mosaic "Mona Lisa of the Galilee." Detail from "Dionysus' Feast"

Cana, the Greek Orthodox
and Melchite Churches

Inserts below:
Left: The crypt in the Church
of the Miracle, with the Jar.
Right: Painting showing Jesus at the
wedding in Cana,
in the Church of the Miracle.

Cana

It was in Cana that Jesus performed His first miracle, changing water into wine at a wedding where He, His mother and His disciples were guests (John 2). *"This beginning of miracles did Jesus in Cana of Galilee, and manifested forth his glory; and his disciples believed on him"* (John 2:11).

There are two churches in Cana, a Greek Orthodox church and the Franciscan Church of the Miracle, which was built in 1879 over the ruins of a sixth century sanctuary. This was the site of the village synagogue where the wedding is believed to have taken place and young couples still come today to celebrate their marriages here. Excavations have revealed an inscription of a dedication written in Aramaic, buried in the mosaic floor, proving that this was indeed the site of the synagogue. In the crypt is an ancient pitcher reputed to be a replica of one of the six original jars used to hold water at the time of the miracle.

The chapel of St. Bartholomew is dedicated to Nathaniel, a native of Cana who was initially skeptical of Jesus, saying: *"Can anything good come out of Nazareth?"* (John 1:46).

The good shepherd

Mosaic of a dedication inscription in the Wedding Church, dating from the fifth century synagogue that once stood here.

Nain - a little over 3 kilometers south of Mt. Tabor is the peaceful village of Nain ("Beauty"). Here Jesus performed the miracle of restoring the widow's son to life. Luke 7:11-15

Opposite Insert: Statue of His Holiness Pope Paul VI who visited the Holy Land

MOUNT TABOR

Mount Tabor

Mount Tabor is not mentioned by name in the Gospels, but according to tradition is the "high mountain apart" which Jesus ascended with the apostles Peter, James and John and where He *"was transfigured before them. And his raiment became shining, exceeding white as snow; so as no fuller on earth can white them"* (Mark 9:2-3).

There is a magnificent view of all the Lower Galilee from the summit of Mount Tabor, which is 660 meters high. The psalmist mentions it with Mount Hermon to illustrate the magnificence of God's creation (Psalm 89:13). In the

Entrance to the site

Ancient mosaic floor

Tympan from the fourth century Basilica on Mount Tabor

time of the Judges, at Deborah's behest, "Barak went down from Mount Tabor and ten thousand men after him" (Judges 4:14) to fight Sisera, captain of the army of the king of Hazor. This was one of the first large battles fought by the Israelites during their conquest of the land. Josephus Flavius, who for a time commanded the Jewish forces in Galilee against the Romans in 66 A.D., writes of the citadel on Mount Tabor, and the strong fortress walls encircling the hill can still be traced.

The first churches were built on Mount Tabor in around 400 A.D. In the time of the Crusaders, a strongly fortified monastery was built by the Benedictines, who managed to

The Greek Orthodox Church of St Elias, built in 1911

Crusader capital
from Mount Tabor

pillars into naves, the central one terminating in a semicircular apse. The dome of the apse features a beautiful golden mosaic depicting the Transfiguration. Christ is in the center surrounded by the prophets Moses and Elijah and Peter, James and John are depicted below. Three enclosed chapels commemorate Peter's proposal to build three tabernacles, one each for Jesus, Moses and Elijah. The Grotto of Christ is at the eastern end of the church and the Elijah and Moses chapels are located in the towers. The Franciscans have also built a large monastery and hospice.

At the entrance to the site is the Crusader Gate of the Winds, which was once surrounded by a protective ditch

withstand attacks by Saladin. However, after the defeat at the Horns of Hittin in 1187, the monks were forced to abandon the site. The Franciscans resettled it in the seventeenth century and they remain there to this day.

The Basilica of the Transfiguration, built by Antonio Barluzzi in the Roman-Syrian style of the 4th-7th centuries, was consecrated in 1924. Among its outstanding features is the facade of two massive towers linked by a large Byzantine-style arch. The interior is divided by three

The present church
built on the ruins
of the Byzantine and Crusader churches

The Basilica of the Transfiguration

Sunclock

crossed by a drawbridge. Northwest of the Franciscan church are the ruins of a large Benedictine monastery of the Crusader period, of which the foundations of the central hall and refectory can still be seen. The ruins of the Greek Orthodox Church and Monastery of Elijah are on the northern part of the mountain and nearby is a chapel known as the Cave of Melchizedek, commemorating the encounter between the patriarch Abraham and Melchizedek (Genesis 14).

Interior of the Basilica of the Transfiguration

Chapel of Moses

Chapel of Elijah the Prophet

Interior of the Basilica of the Transfiguration

Capernaum

At the time of Jesus, Capernaum was a wealthy Jewish town. Here Jesus met His first disciples Peter, Andrew, James, John and Matthew, all fishermen who worked on the Sea of Galilee. Jesus performed many miracles in Capernaum and the surrounding area. Here He healed Peter's wife's mother of a fever, brought a child back to life, cured a leper, healed the centurion's servant and *"cast out the spirits with his word, and healed all that were sick"* (Matthew 8:16). Among His many teachings here were the parable of the sower, of tares among the wheat, of a grain of mustard seed, of the treasure hidden in the field and of the fishing net. However, the people of Capernaum did not believe in Jesus and he consequently cursed them: *"And thou, Capernaum, which art exalted unto heaven, shalt be brought down to hell"* (Matthew 11:23).

The ruins of the white limestone synagogue from around 300 A.D., built in the typical basilica style, are believed to stand on the site of the original synagogue in which Jesus preached during His ministry in Galilee. Its carved lintels are richly decorated with Jewish symbols such as the menorah (seven-branched candelabrum), shofar (ram's horn) and the carriage carrying the Ark of the Covenant.

Partial view of the ancient synagogue

Bird's eye view of Capernaum and the Sea of Galilee, showing the new church covering Peter's house and the family living quarters.

The modern new church

Insert: Laying the corner-stone ▲
for the new church ⋮

Model
of the house
of St. Peter ◄ ⋯⋯⋯⋯

Interior
of the ▼
new church

The traditional house of St. Peter, one of a group of houses, was discovered beneath the remains of the Byzantine octagonal church. A new church has been built over the site but it is generally kept closed and only opened by special request for groups of pilgrims who wish to celebrate Mass.

Remains of the ancient
synagogue on which
Jewish symbols
are carved.

A relief
from the synagogue
showing a Star of David

A relief from the synagogue
showing the carriage for carrying
the Holy Ark of the Covenant.

On the left of the picture is a mill for crushing olives,
and to the right an oil press which can also be used to make flour.

The exterior of the Church of the Multiplication of the Loaves and the Fishes

TABGHA

The courtyard of the Church of the Multiplication of the Loaves and the Fishes ·····················▶

Bird's eye view of Tabgha ; left: the Church of the Multiplication - right: the Church of St. Peter.

The name Tabgha is a distortion of the Greek word Heptapegon, which means 'Seven Springs'. In the past, seven springs met at this point and flowed into the Sea of Galilee, however today only five remain. This is the traditional site of the Miracle of the Loaves and Fishes which Jesus performed in order to feed the multitudes who had come to hear Him preach: *"But Jesus said unto them. They need not depart: give ye them to eat. And they say unto Him, We have here but five loaves, and two fishes. He said, Bring them hither to me. And He commanded the multitude to sit down on the grass, and took the five loaves and the two fishes, and looking up to heaven, he blessed, and brake, and gave the loaves to His disciples, and the disciples to the multitude. And they did all eat, and were filled: and they took up the fragments that remained twelve baskets full. And they that had eaten were about five thousand men, besides women and children."* (Matthew 14:16-21)

The table rock where this miracle took place has been the altar of successive churches, the earliest built in the fourth century and replaced a century later by a larger structure. The mosaic pavement still remains in the modern church, which was built in 1982 for the German Benedictines in Byzantine style. The mosaic in front of the altar symbolizes the loaves and fishes, and in the transept are beautiful mosaics depicting water birds and plants.

The Loaves and the Fishes

Part of the Byzantine mosaic floor

Part of the Byzantine mosaic floor

The interior of the Church of the Multiplication

One of the seven springs in Tabgha

◄ ....

DALMANUTHA

After the miracle at Tabgha, Jesus *"entered into a ship with his disciples, and came into the parts of Dalmanutha"* (Mark 8:10). Traditionally, this is where Jesus sighed for mankind. The place of meditation, on the west side of the Sea of Galilee near Magdala, is marked with a great Cross facing the peaceful waters.

Dalmanutha prayer site, on the western side of the Sea of Galilee

The Church of St. Peter's Primacy

Nearby, along the shore, is the Church of St. Peter's Primacy or Mensa Christi - the Table of Christ. This chapel, whose simplicity is enhanced by the black basalt rocks used in its construction, marks the place where Jesus appeared for the third time after His death: *"When the morning was now come, Jesus stood on the shore: but the disciples knew not that it was Jesus ... This is now the third time that Jesus shewed himself to his disciples, after that he was risen from the dead"* (John 21:4,14).

Here they ate together and here Jesus appointed Simon Peter to the office of the Primacy with the words *"Feed my lambs ... feed my sheep"* (John 21:15,19). The church was built by the Franciscans in 1934 on Byzantine foundations and the rock emerging from the center of the floor is the "table" at which they ate. The church is located on a small quay with rock-hewn steps on which Jesus is said to have stood as he looked over the water.

The Church of St Peter's Primacy overlooking the Sea of Galilee

*Pilgrims outside the Church
of St Peter's Primacy*

*Statue overlooking the Sea of Galilee.
This statue depicts Christ after the Resurrection,
appearing before his disciples for the third time.*

Interior of the Church of St Peter's Primacy

The Church of the Beatitudes

View of the Sea of Galilee from the Church of the Beatitudes

Situated atop the Mount of Beatitudes overlooking the Sea of Galilee, the octagonal shaped chapel of the Church of the Beatitudes marks the spot where Jesus preached the Sermon on the Mount: *"And seeing the multitude he went up into a mountain ... and he opened his mouth, and taught them"* (Matthew 5:1-2). Remains of a small Byzantine church were discovered here in 1935, but the Franciscans chose to rebuild the modern church on the hilltop, not over the ancient chapel. Constructed by Antonio Barluzzi of local basalt, with a colonnaded cloister of white stone surrounding it, the octagonal church recalls the eight blessings, one of which is inscribed on each wall. The mosaic on the floor is decorated with symbols of the virtues of man referred to in the sermon.

*View of the Sea of Galilee
and the Church of the Beatitudes*

The high altar in the Church of the Beatitudes

"*Blessed are the poor in spirit: for theirs is the kingdom of heaven.*

Blessed are they that mourn: for they shall be comforted.

Blessed are the meek: for they shall inherit the earth.

Blessed are they which do hunger and thirst after righteousness: for they shall be filled.

Blessed are the merciful: for they shall obtain mercy.

Blessed are the poor in heart: for they shall see God.

Blessed are the peacemakers: for they shall be called the children of God.

Blessed are they which are persecuted for righteousness' sake: for theirs is the kingdom of heaven."

Matthew 5:3-10

BEATI MVNDO
CORDE
QVONIAM IPSI
DEVM VIDEBVNT

BEATI QVI
LVGENT
QVONIAM IPSI
CONSOLABVNTVR

BEATI PAVPERES
SPIRITV
QVONIAM IPSORVM
EST REGNVM COELORVM

BEATI MITES
QVONIAM IPSI POS-
SIDEBVNT TERRAM

BEATI QVI PERSECVTIONEM
PATIVNTVR PROPTER
IVSTITIAM QVIAM IPSVM
EST REGNVM CCELVM

BEATI PACIFICI
QVONIAM FILII
DEI VOCABVNTVR

BEATI MISERI-
CORDES
QVONIAM IPSI MISERI-
CORDIAM CONSEQVENTVR

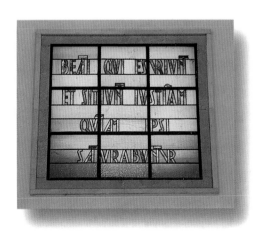

BEATI QVI ESVRIVNT
ET SITIVNT IVSTIAM
QVIAM IPSI
SATVRABVNTVR

Church of the Miracle of the Swine.

Korazin

The Jews of the thriving town of Korazin refused to allow Jesus to preach there and He cursed them: *"Woe unto thee, Chorazin! woe unto thee Bethsaida! . . . it shall be more tolerable for Tyre and Sidon at the judgment, than for you".* (Luke 10:13-14)

Today all that remains of Korazin are the ruins of the black basalt second century A.D synagogue. Korazin seems to have been destroyed by an earthquake in the third century and was never rebuilt.

Kursi

Kursi is the New Testament Gergesa, or Gadara, where Jesus met the two men possessed of devils. He cast the devils into a herd of swine, which stampeded into the Sea of Galilee and was drowned. The site of the miracle was not known until the late 1960's when the ruins of a Byzantine basilica with a mosaic floor were by chance discovered.

View towards Bethsaida

The Galilee Boat
from the time of Jesus,
now preserved and
housed in a museum

Remains of the ancient
synagogue of Korazin

Insert: Mosaic from Magdala
depicting an ancient boat

FIRST CENT.
A.D.
MAGDALA

Caesarea Philippi

"When Jesus came into the coasts of Caesarea Philippi, he asked his disciples saying. Whom do men say that I the Son of man am?...and Simon Peter answered and said, Thou are the Christ, the Son of the living god. And Jesus answered: Blessed art thou, Simon, son of John...for thou art Peter and upon this rock [Petrus] I will build my church" (Matthew 16). Jesus gave Peter the keys to the kingdom of heaven, saying "whatsoever thou shalt bind on earth shall be bound in heaven" (Matthew 16:19).

At the time of Jesus, Caesarea Philippi was a fruitful glen through which a river flowed, with opulent residences, colonnaded streets and large temples. The city was given to Herod by the Roman emperor Augustus and as a token of his gratitude, he built a palace to Caesar. After Herod's death, his son Philip embellished the city and made it his capital, renaming it Caesarea Philippi. The present name dates from the seventh-century Arab conquest and back to the ancient Greek name Panias. Lacking the letter "P" in their alphabet, Arab pronunciation became "Banias".

Ruins of the ancient town of Susita ▶

Yardenit - Place of Baptism

Countless pilgrims from far and wide gather at Yardenit, where the River Jordan leaves the Sea of Galilee, to immerse themselves in the holy waters of the River Jordan. Clad in white robes, they are devoutly following in the tradition of the scriptures: Jesus *"was baptized of John in Jordan "(Mark 1:9).* The Yardenit site was developed by Kibbutz Kinneret, and facilities provided for pilgrims wishing to participate in baptism ceremonies.

MOUNT GILBOA

"*T*he beauty of Israel is slain upon thy high places: how are the mighty fallen ... Ye mountains of Gilboa, let there be no dew, neither let there be rain" (II Samuel 1:19).

Thus David lamented Saul and Jonathon at the foot of Mount Gilboa after they were killed here in battle by the Philistines.

Mount Gilboa

The baptismal site on the River Jordan

A painting of the baptism of Jesus is to be found at St. John the Baptist Church in Ein Karem

Pilgrims participating in a ceremony at the spot where Jesus was baptized in the River Jordan

The Mount of Temptation

"And immediately the Spirit driveth him into the wilderness. And he was there in the wilderness forty days, tempted of Satan; and was with the wild beasts; and the angels ministered unto him" (Mark 1:12-13).

O n the side of a mountain west of Jericho is the Greek Orthodox Monastery called the Monastery of Quarantel (from the Latin for "forty days") or the Monastery of the Temptation. According to tradition, it was here that Jesus isolated Himself and fasted for forty days, resisting the Devil's offer of *"all the kingdoms in the world"* (Luke 4:5).

At the top of the mountain are the remains of a chapel, which marks the spot where Satan tempted Jesus.

During the Byzantine period, hermits inhabited the area, living in caves. The present-day monastery was built at the end of the nineteenth century with funds donated by the Russian Church. It was carved out of the mountainside halfway up and built partly in the rock over the chasm. Today it is inhabited only by a few monks.

The Monastery of Temptation

The stone of Temptation on which Jesus is said to have sat.

The Mount of Temptation (Jebel Quarantel)

Jericho, as depicted in the Byzantine mosaic Medaba map.

Jericho

Jericho, also known as the "City of Palms", is one of the oldest cities in the world and ancient Jericho - Tel-es-Sultan - was the first place where man settled permanently, abandoning the wandering life-style of the herdsman. The Children of Israel crossed the River Jordan nearby and in 1250 B.C the city fell to the blast of Joshua's trumpets. Elijah was taken to Heaven from Jericho, and here Elisha purified the water with salt. The Greek Orthodox Church of St. Elisha commemorates this miracle.

On His way to Jerusalem, Jesus passed through Jericho. Amongst the crowd of people waiting to catch a glimpse of Him was a small man named Zaccheus. In order to get a better view, he climbed into a sycomore tree. The story of how Zaccheus received salvation is told in Luke 19:5-9.

The spring of Elisha (Ain es Sultan)

Excavations at the ancient Tel es Sultan with the Mt. of Temptation in the background.

The sycomore tree of Jericho

The Hulda Steps in the southern wall of the Temple Mount. These led into the courtyard at the time of the Second Temple and were the very steps used by Jesus.

◄ ....

"*A*nd he brought him to Jerusalem, and set him on a pinnacle of the temple, and said unto him, If thou be the Son of God, cast thyself down from hence...And Jesus answering said unto him, it is said, Thou shalt not tempt the Lord thy God" (Luke 4:9,12).

The pinnacle of the Temple in Jerusalem to which Satan brought Jesus in order to tempt him for the third time.

Qumran

The most exciting archaeological find of this century took place in 1947 when two young Bedouin shepherds, searching for a lost goat, accidentally discovered a hoard of ancient manuscripts in a cave at Qumran. Over 2000 years ago, Qumran, which is situated at the lowest point of the earth's surface in the Great Rift Valley, was a flourishing settlement. Here, between 150 B.C. and 68 A.D., the community of the Essenes found an ideally secluded place for prayer and contemplation. Exiled from the temptations of the city, high up on a limestone plateau overlooking the Dead Sea, they awaited the coming of the Lord, according to their interpretation of the words of the prophet Isaiah (Isaiah 40:3).

When the ruins of the site were cleared, a complete Essene monastery was found with a large Assembly Hall

*Two fragments
from the Dead Sea
Scrolls found
at Qumran,
with an inkpot
of the
Roman period*

The caves of Qumran

*One of the jars in which the scrolls
were originally stored (Cave 1)*

and dining room, kitchens and laundry, cisterns, ritual baths and vast scriptorium where the Essenes transcribed Biblical and other texts on leather, papyrus and copper scrolls. When Titus and the Roman legions arrived at Jericho, the Essenes fled, hiding their scrolls in the nearby caves. The desert kept their secret for almost 2000 years. The discovery of the scrolls had an enormous effect on the Christian world as they were transcribed during the time of the birth of Christianity. Many of the scrolls discovered at Qumran are now housed in the Shrine of the Book at the Israel Museum in Jerusalem.

The excavated ruins of the buildings that stood here before the site was abandoned in the first century A.D.

One of the great cisterns.

Cracked steps leading to a ritual bath, caused by the earthquakes of 31 B.C.

◄ ....

Ein Gedi

"And David went up from thence, and dwelt in the strongholds at Ein Gedi" (Samuel I :23-29).

Ein Gedi is an ancient settlement near the shores of the Dead Sea and is famous for its springs and waterfalls. It was one of the desert settlements of the Tribe of Judah and it was to Ein Gedi that David fled from Saul.

Ein Gedi means "Spring of the Young Goat", and many ibexes - mountain goats - are to be found in the Judean Desert, especially around the caves and cliffs of Ein Gedi.

Crystallized mounds
of salt on the shores
of the Dead Sea

*"But his wife looked back
from behind him, and she
become a pillar of salt".*
Genesis 19:26

The rock-pillar known as "Lot's wife"

Masada

Masada, situated above the Dead Sea, was one of the fortresses luxuriously built and fortified by Herod the Great. Approach was difficult. The only way seems to have been by the narrow Snake Path, tortuously winding up the eastern slope of the mountain. At Masada, the few surviving Jewish patriots who took part in the Jewish Revolt against the Romans gathered in 70 A.D. to make their last stand. The Zealots, led by Eleazar ben Yair, were besieged for three years by the Romans. Realizing that it was impossible to hold out any longer, the 967 defenders committed suicide preferring to die as free men rather than be taken into captivity by the Romans. Excavations led by the late Professor Yigael Yadin uncovered the remains of the fortress with its storerooms, cisterns, bathhouses, palaces, synagogue and ritual baths. The touching remains of the Zealots' last days - the lettered sherds with which they cast lots, the tattered raiment, the sandals and the plaits of women's hair - are displayed in the Israel Museum.

The Byzantine church built in the 6th century A.D.

An aerial view of the fortress-hill of Masada.

Insert: The caldarium (Hot room) in the bath-house adjoining the northern palace.

JERUSALEM

"If I forget thee, O Jerusalem, let my right hand forget her cunning" (Psalm 137:5)

"Thus saith the Lord God; this is Jerusalem: I have set it in the midst of the nations and countries that are round about her" (Ezekiel 5:5).

"Beautiful for situation, the joy of the whole earth, is Mount Zion...the city of the great King" (Psalm 48:2)

References and quotations about Jerusalem in the Bible are innumerable. It is known as the Sacred City, Jerusalem the Golden, the City of Peace, the City of David, Zion. . . There is not another city that has been the cause of so many armed conflicts as Jerusalem. Its holy sites, revered by the three great monotheistic faiths, are a constant draw to pilgrims from all over the world.

Jerusalem, the Old City

Bethany

"*N*ow a certain man was sick, named Lazarus, of Bethany, the town of Mary and her sister Martha... When Jesus heard that, he said, This sickness is not unto death, but for the glory of God, that the Son of God might be glorified thereby" (John 11:1-4)

Entrance to the Tomb of Lazarus

◄ ···

The Tomb of Lazarus

The Church of St. Lazarus

Jesus raising Lazarus from the dead.

On the eastern slope of the Mount of Olives is the Arab village of El Azariya. This is the ancient Bethany, which Jesus passed on His way from Jericho to Jerusalem. Here Jesus performed the miracle of raising Lazarus, brother of Martha and Mary, from the dead. Lazarus' grave is behind the Franciscan Sanctuary of St. Lazarus, a masterpiece built in 1954 by the Italian architect Barluzzi on the ruins of previous churches. Inside the church are many mosaics, copies of frescoes painted by G. Vagarini.

Above the church is a ruined tower, said to be on the site of Simon the Leper's house, where Jesus sat when a woman anointed him with precious spikenard and his fellow guests complained of the waste: *"Why trouble ye the woman?" And Jesus said: "For she hath wrought good work upon me "* (Matthew 26:10).

The interior of the Church of St Lazarus

A mill-stone in the Church of St Lazarus

Bethphage

Bethphage, on the slopes of the Mount of Olives, is closely associated with the last days of Jesus. Jesus sent two of his disciples to Bethphage to fetch a young ass for him to ride when entering Jerusalem amid waving palm branches. *"...When they heard that Jesus was coming to Jerusalem, Took branches of palm trees, and went forth to meet him, and cried, Hosanna: Blessed is the King of Israel that cometh in the name of the Lord. And Jesus, when he had found a young ass, rode thereon: as it is written, "* (John 12:12-14).

A fresco above the main altar of the Church at Bethphage shows the entry of Jesus into Jerusalem. A stone in the Church is said to bear the imprint of Jesus' foot as He mounted the ass. It is from here that the Palm Sunday procession begins, ending at the Church of St Anne in the Old City.

The Palm Sunday procession starting from the Church of Bethphage on its way to Jerusalem.

Frescos showing a Palm Sunday procession in the Crusader Chapel at Bethphage, the Mount of Olives (XII Century)

A fresco above the main altar of the church at Bethphage which shows the entry of Jesus into Jerusalem riding on a young ass.

The Church of the Pater Noster

The Church of the Pater Noster, or Eleona, was originally built in the fourth century by Empress Helena, mother of Constantine. A cavern where Jesus taught the Lord's Prayer is now a chapel, and the Carmelite cloister is lined with glazed tiles bearing the text of the prayer in more than sixty languages, including braille.

The Carmelite Chapel built in 1874.
·····························▶

Right below: Tomb of the Princesse de la Tour d'Auvergne (Aurelie de Bossi)

·····························▶

The Grotto of the Eschatological Teachings where, according to tradition, Jesus taught the disciples the Lord's Prayer. Here, during the first six centuries A.D., the Patriarchs of Jerusalem were buried.

Cloister of the Pater Noster Church

Mount of Olives

For Christianity, no mountain holds more far-reaching importance and sentiment than Olivet, or the mount of Olives; nowhere did Jesus spend more time during his mission in Jerusalem. When Jesus was in the area, he would stay with his friends at Bethany and on his way to and from the city he would pass through the Mount of Olives. Here, overlooking the Temple, he taught his disciples, prophesied the destruction of Jerusalem and wept over its fate (Luke 19:37-41). On its slopes, in the Garden of Gethsemane, he was taken captive, and from its summit he ascended. In antiquity, the Mount was indeed covered with olive trees but the Romans cut most of them down to build the rampart for the siege of Jerusalem during the Great Revolt of the Jews in 70 A.D.

The mountain is first mentioned in the Bible when King David, fleeing from Absalom, "went up by the ascent of Mount Olivet "(II Sam. 15:30). During Second Temple times, Jewish pilgrims would bring their red heifers here to be burnt for the ashes of purification (Lev. 16; Heb. 9:13) and signal fires were lit at the new moon to inform Jews of the new month's coming. Here Ezechiel viewed the heavenly chariots and Zechariah prophecied the End of Days: *"And his feet shall stand in that day upon the mount of Olives"* (Zec. 14:4) ushering in everlasting peace. Legend tells that the Messiah will enter the Temple Courts through the now-blocked Golden Gate opposite the mountain. For this reason, pious Jews have throughout the ages chosen to be buried here so as to be among the first to follow the Messiah on the Day of Redemption.

The procession entering St. Stephen's Gate

The Palm Sunday procession starting from Bethphage on its way to Jerusalem.

When the procession reaches Jerusalem, the assembled pilgrims join the prayer.

The Dome of Ascension

The small Dome of Ascension stands in the center of an octagonal courtyard. From this spot, Jesus ascended to heaven forty days after His Resurrection. The chapel today functions as a mosque but the various Christian denominations are permitted to celebrate the Feast of Ascension forty days after Easter and their altars stand in the courtyard. The first church was built here at the end of the fourth century and a seventh century pilgrim describes it as having two rows of pillars with arches, a rotunda and the footprint of Jesus inside the Chapel. The Persians destroyed this church and in the twelfth century, the Crusaders built a new church, part of which stands today: their decorated capitals with typical motifs of griffins and floral designs are well-preserved. After they recaptured Jerusalem, the Moslems converted it into a mosque, blocking up the openings between the pillars and arches and closing the cupola. The footprint of Jesus is in a rectangular stone frame.

The Chapel of the Ascension

The footprint of Jesus inside the Chapel of the Ascension

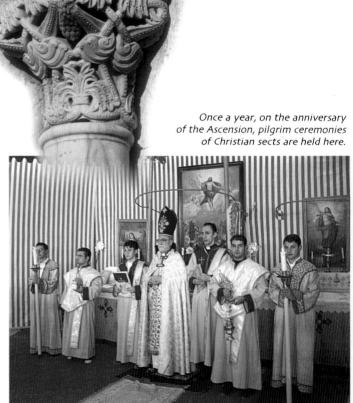

Once a year, on the anniversary of the Ascension, pilgrim ceremonies of Christian sects are held here.

The City of David

Excavations on the site of David's city have brought to light part of the Jebusite ramparts of 4000 years ago, Israelite houses and fortifications from the time of King David, as well as later walls and towers.   Part of the underground water system, also still remains and is known as Warren's Shaft after the British archeologist who discovered it in 1867. This shaft gave the population of Israelite Jerusalem access to the waters of the Gihon Spring even in times of war. Excavations have revealed remains of Canaanite settlements from before the time of King David, houses from the period of Judah's kings and remnants of what may have been David's citadel.

Right below:
Remains of channels
in the City of David,
quarried to deliver water
to fields in the Kidron Valley.

The stepped stone structure that
supported a large building in the City of
David , perhaps David's palace.
···►

Warren's Shaft

Mount Zion

In the time of the Old Testament, Mount Zion was the name given to the City of David: *'David took the strong hold of Zion; the same is the city of David "* (II Samuel 5:7).

However by Jesus' time, almost one thousand years later, a monument to David's tomb had migrated to the present Mount Zion. The tomb fell into ruin in 133 A.D. but was accidentally rediscovered in 1158 and is venerated to this day by Christians, Jews and Moslems.

On the tomb are silver crowns from Torah scrolls brought to Israel from synagogues in the Diaspora which were destroyed together with their communities during the Holocaust. Jews come to pray at the Tomb of David throughout the year, but especially at Shavuot (The Feast of Weeks), the date of David's death.

The traditional Tomb of King David

Mount Zion

The Church of Hagia Maria Zion
(The Dormition)

The octagonal Church of the Dormition, which towers above Mount Zion, commemorates the tradition that here the Virgin Mary fell into eternal sleep. In 383, the Byzantines built the Church of the Column here, placing the Flagellation post within it. In 415, John II, Bishop of Jerusalem, enlarged this church calling it Hagia Sion - Holy Zion. It is this church, called the mother of all churches, that is shown on the sixth century Medaba map found in Jordan. The Hagia Zion Church was destroyed in 614 by the Persians and rebuilt by the Crusaders who named it Our Lady of Zion and incorporated in it the Room of the Last Supper. The present church was built at the beginning of the twentieth century by German Benedictines on the remains of the previous churches, and they still run the church and abbey. The beautiful mosaic floor in the church depicts the Holy Trinity, the apostles and the zodiac.

A staircase leads down from the upper church to the crypt venerated as Mary's home after the Resurrection, and as the place of her death. In the center of the crypt is a life-size statue of the sleeping Mary made of cherry wood and ivory and in the dome above, a mosaic depicting the figure of Christ welcoming his mother, surrounded by six famous women of the Old Testament.

The crypt
The Hagia Maria Zion Sanctuary

The Coenaculum

The Coenaculum, or Cenacle, is the *"large upper room furnished and prepared"* where Jesus and His disciples ate the Passover feast, the Last Supper (Mark 14). The present structure is a fourteenth century renovation with Gothic windows and Crusader arches.

Detail of capital in the Cenacle, Mt Zion

The Coenaculum (Cenacle), room of the Last Supper

The Kidron Valley

It is traditionally believed that when the Universal Resurrection is completed, trumpets will sound and the Last Judgment will take place in the Kidron Valley. For this reason the site has been a favored burial place for Jews for thousands of years.

The Kidron Valley - The Tombs of Absalom, Bnei Hezir and St. James are starkly illuminated against the blackness of the night.

Dominus Flevit

The Church of Dominus Flevit on the slopes of the Mount of Olives, facing the Temple Mount, marks the spot where Jesus wept over the fate of the city of Jerusalem, which would shortly be destroyed: *"thine enemies...shall lay thee even with the ground and thy children within thee; they shall not leave within thee one stone upon another"* (Luke 19:41-44). The present church was built on the ruins of an ancient church.

The Jewish cemetery on the Mount of Olives

The Church of Dominus Flevit on the slopes of the Mount of Olives, facing the Temple Mount.

Ossuary in Dominus Flevit

The window above the altar through which the Temple Mount and Jerusalem can be seen.

Ancient olive trees in the Garden of Gethsemane ....▶

Gethsemane

On the lower slopes of the Mount of Olives there stands to this day a stately grove of eight ancient olive trees. These trees and their fruit have given this site their name, Gethsemane: gat-shamna is olive-press in Aramaic. The garden is well-kept by the Franciscan brothers. It was here, to Gethsemane, that Jesus came to pray with His disciples.

The Basilica of the Agony

Also known as the Church of All Nations, for it was sponsored jointly by several countries, the Basilica of the Agony was built by the Italian architect Barluzzi over the remains of two earlier churches. Jesus and His disciples spent the last hours before His arrest in the Garden of Gethsemane and the mosaic on the front facade depicts Him offering up both His and the world's sufferings *"who in the days of his flesh, when he had offered up prayers and supplications with strong crying and tears"* (Hebrews 5:7). Within the Church is the Rock of Agony upon which Jesus prayed and sweated blood the night before His arrest. The rock is surrounded by a crown of thorns of wrought iron.

The Basilica of the Agony and the Russian Orthodox Church on the slopes of the Mount of Olives.
◄ ....

The Rock of the Agony

The cupola of the Church of All Nations

Angel from Gethsemane

Icon in the Church

The Church of the Tomb of the Virgin Mary

A majestic staircase descends to the crypt where Mary was buried and then taken up to heaven. This candle-lit cave, which was built by the Crusaders, is today in the hands of the Armenian and Greek Orthodox churches. In the church are altars dedicated to Joachim and Anne, the Virgin Mary's parents. Queen Melisanda, who reigned here during the Crusader period, is also buried here.

The Church of the Tomb of the Virgin Mary.

The Russian Church of Mary Magdalene

Interior
of the Church

The Russian Church of Mary Magdalene was built in 1888 by Czar Alexander III. The golden domes are typical of the Muscovite church style.

*Pottery found
at the Pool of Siloam*

The Pool of Siloam

The Pool of Siloam

In biblical times, the Gihon spring was Jerusalem's only water supply and when enemies were at the gate, the first priority was the safety of the spring. King Hezekiah built the Silwan Tunnel, also known as Hezekiah's Tunnel, in around 700 B.C. to bring water directly into the town. An inscription in ancient Hebrew script, found chiselled into the conduit wall, commemorates the meeting of Hezekiah's two work gangs who began at each end of the tunnel and met midway.

The water of the Pool of Siloam, being pure spring water from the Gihon Spring, was used for ceremonies in the Temple. It was to this pool that Jesus sent the blind man to wash after he had covered his eyes with a mixture of clay and spittle: *"And he said unto him. Go, wash in the Pool of Siloam. He went his way therefore, and washed, and came seeing"* (John 9:7).

Hezekiah's workers cut the tunnel through the rock in order to bring the waters of the Gihon Spring inside the City walls in time of siege.

A Hebrew inscription, on display at the Istanbul Archaeological Museum, describes the construction of Hezekiah's Tunnel.

Stained-glass window

An ancient flight of steps leads up to the church and is believed to be those trodden by Jesus on his way to be tried at the House of Caiphas.

The Church of St. Peter in Gallicantu

The Church of St. Peter in Gallicantu stands on the site of the house of Caiphas the High Priest at the time of Jesus. This is traditionally where Peter denied his Master, according to the prophecy of Jesus: *"Before the cock crow twice, thou shalt deny me thrice".* (Mark 14:66-72)

Beneath the Church

The cupola

Interior of the Church

Bas-relief next to ancient stepped street: After the Last Supper, "Jesus left the Cenacle with his disciples and crossed the Kidron Valley". (John 18.1)

The Pools of Bethesda

I n 1871, excavations carried out close to St. Anne's Church uncovered the remains of two large rectangular pools. These are the Pools of Bethesda, as described in John 5:2. Here Jesus performed the miracle of

Byzantine lamps with Cross and doves, 7th Century. St Anne Collection.

The Church of St Anne & Pools of Bethesda

healing a crippled man. Colonnades divide the pool into sections. It is believed that sheep were washed in one of these pools before they were sacrificed in the Temple.

The Church of St. Anne

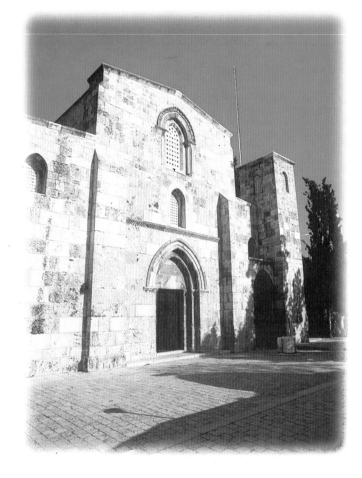

The Church of St. Anne is one of the best-preserved and finest examples of a church built during the Crusader period. It is located near St. Stephen's Gate and is built over a crypt venerated as the birthplace of the Virgin Mary and the home of her parents Anne and Joachim. When Saladin conquered Jerusalem, he turned the building into an Islamic school, but after the Ottoman conquest it was abandoned. Today the White Fathers use it as a Greek Seminary.

Roman marble figurine, from the excavations at St. Anne's Pool.

Chapel of the Crypt

Interior of the Basilica of St. Anne

VIA DOLOROSA
The Stations of the Cross

First Station: Jesus is condemned.

Jesus was tried and condemned by Pontius Pilate in the Praetorium, the Antonia Fortress, headquarters of the Roman garrison stationed in Jerusalem and residence of the procurator when he visited Jerusalem. Today, the First Station is in the courtyard of the Al-Omariya school.

Interior of the Second Station of the Cross

The Franciscan Chapel of the Flagellation and Chapel of Condemnation.
Facade of the Chapel of the Flagellation

"And straightaway in the morning the chief priests held a consultation with the elders and scribes and the whole council, and bound Jesus and carried him away, and delivered him to Pilate" (Mark 15:1).

Second Station: Jesus takes up the Cross

The Franciscan Chapel of the Flagellation and Chapel of Condemnation commemorate the sites where Jesus was scourged and given the Cross to bear.

"And the soldiers platted a crown of thorns, and put it on his head, and they put on him a purple robe, and said, Hail, King of the Jews! And they smote him with their hands" (John 19:2-3).

Interior of the Dome of the Convent of the Flagellation.

"Pilate brought Jesus forth and sat down in the judgment seat in a place that is called the Pavement, but in the Hebrew Gabbatha".
(John 19:13)

The Dome of the Chapel of the Lithostrotos. The Chapel marks the Second Station of the Via Dolorosa. It is located in the Antonia Fortress where Pontius Pilate judged Jesus in a place called Gabbatha (pavement). John 19:13

Opposite above: Part of the pavement in the courtyard of the Antonia Fortress, in the Convent of the "Sisters of Zion".
◄ ....

Lithostrotos: The Stone Pavement

The vaulted basement of the Convent of the Sisters of Zion covers the remains of an ancient Roman pavement, Lithostrotos, made of large flagstones specially etched to prevent horses from slipping. It probably dates back to the time of Hadrian. On the paving stones are signs of the 'Game of the King' played by the Roman soldiers. Traditionally it is believed that the Place of Judgment was on this pavement which was in the western section of the Antonia Fortress.

◄ ....

Opposite in insert: The Stone of Basilinda - markings on the pavement clearly show evidence of the "King's Game" played by the Roman legionaries.

Arch in Jerash (Jordan) similar to the one that once stood here.
.... ►

Painting of the "Ecce Homo" Arch
The "Ecce Homo" Arch

Ecce Homo Arch

The Ecce Homo Arch is part of the eastern entrance to the Roman city Aelia Capitolina, constructed by Hadrian as a triumphal arch with three portals. According to tradition, this is the spot where Pontius Pilate ordered Jesus to be brought forth to the Jews, proclaiming "Ecce Homo" (Behold the Man). Today, the left-hand, smaller arch is included in the Chapel of the Ecce Homo in the Convent of the Sisters of Zion. The larger arch spans part of the Via Dolorosa.

◄ ....
Model of the Antonia Fortress which was built by Herod the Great in 36 B.C. in honor of his friend Mark Antony. It was destroyed by Titus in 70 A.D.

Third Station
Jesus falls for the first time

An Armenian Catholic chapel marks the spot where Jesus fell for the first time and above the entrance there is a relief of Jesus falling under the weight of the Cross.

"The comforter that should relieve my soul is far from me"
(Lamentations 1:16)

4th Station
Jesus meets His mother

The Armenian Church of Our Lady of the Spasm marks the spot where Jesus, carrying the cross, was met by His mother - the Virgin Mary.

"And Simeon blessed them and said unto Mary his mother, Behold, this child is set for the fall and rising again of many in Israel; and for a sign which shall be spoken against" (Luke 2:34)

5th Station
The Cyrenian helps Jesus carry the cross

The Fifth Station is commemorated by a Franciscan chapel. Here the Way of the Cross begins the ascent to Golgotha.

"And as they led him away, they laid hold upon one Simon, a Cyrenian, coming out of the country, and on him they laid the cross, that he might bear it after Jesus". (Luke 23:26)

6th Station
Veronica wipes Jesus' face

According to tradition, the Sixth Station is revered as the place where Jesus was helped by Veronica when she wiped the dust and dirt from His face. The imprint of Jesus' face was left on the cloth that Veronica used, which is preserved at St. Peter's Church in Rome. The Church of St. Veronica belongs to the Little Sisters of Jesus.

"The Lord make his face shine upon thee and be gracious unto thee" Numbers 6:25

7th Station ▲
⋮
9th Station ▼

8th Station ▲
⋮

7th Station
Jesus falls for the second time

Two chapels connected by a flight of steps mark the site where Jesus fell for the second time under the weight of the Cross. Inside the Franciscan chapel there is a Roman pillar on which the written condemnation of Jesus was probably written. It is believed that here was the Gate of Judgment through which Jesus left the city on His way to Golgotha.

"And the angel of his presence saved them: In his love and in his pity he redeemed them". (Isaiah 63:9)

8th Station
Jesus consoles the daughters of Jerusalem

On the wall of the Greek monastery of St. Charalambos is a stone with a Latin cross and an inscription reading "Jesus Christ is victorious". This station is believed to have been located outside the city walls of Jerusalem in the Second Temple period.

"Jesus turning unto them said, Daughters of Jerusalem, weep not for me, but weep for yourselves and for your children". (Luke 23:28)

9th Station
Jesus falls for the third time

A column built into the door of the Coptic church marks the site where Jesus fell for the third time. From this spot He could see the place of crucifixion.

"And he went a little further and fell on his face, and prayed, saying O my Father, if it be possible, let this cup pass from me: nevertheless not as I will but as thou wilt".
(Matthew 26:39)

Russian excavations. Part of the Atrium of Constantine's Church of the Holy Sepulcher.

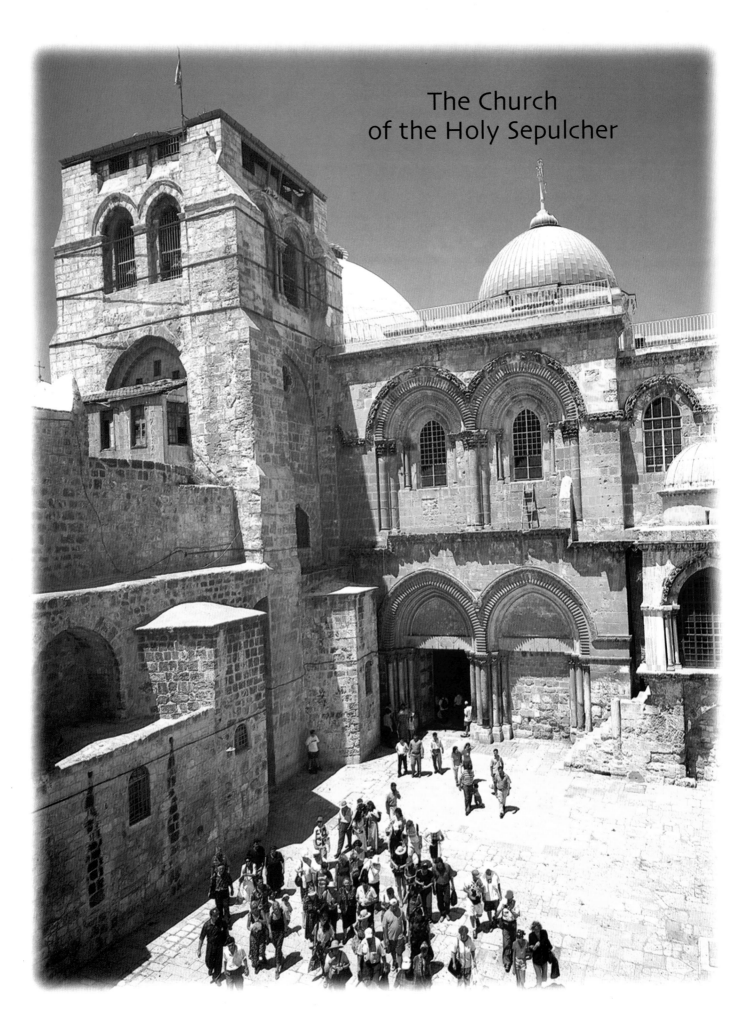

The Church
of the Holy Sepulcher

The Church of the Holy Sepulcher was first built by order of the Emperor Constantine the Great immediately following the Council of Nicaea in 325 A.D. The tomb of Jesus was discovered by the Empress Helena, mother of Constantine, after it had been revealed to her in a dream while she was on a visit to Jerusalem. Three different buildings were erected on the spot: a round church called the Anastasis above the

empty grave of Jesus; a magnificent basilica called the Martyrium; and in the square between the two churches, a shrine marking the position of the crucifixion, named Calvarium (Golgotha). These buildings were destroyed by the Persians in 614. They were rebuilt and once more destroyed by Caliph Hakim in 1009. Then, in 1149, after the conquest of Jerusalem, the Crusaders erected the present church, which contains

the tomb of Jesus and place of crucifixion under one roof. Within the compound are also the Chapel of Adam, the Chapel of St. Helena and the Chapel of the Finding of the Cross.

At the time of Jesus, this site was outside the walls of the city, for Jewish custom forbade execution and burial to be performed within the city.

10th Station
Jesus is stripped of his garments

The last five stations of the Way of the Cross are in the Basilica of the Holy Sepulcher. A small stone stairway leads to the Chapel of the Divestiture.

Calvary ....▶

11th Station
Jesus is nailed to the Cross

Magnificent mosaics decorate the place where Jesus was crucified .

"And when they were come to the place, which is called Calvary, there they crucified him, and the malefactors, one on the right hand and the other on the left".

(Luke 23:33)

12th Station
Jesus dies on the Cross

A Greek Orthodox chapel marks the site of the death of Jesus. The altar is flanked by two supporting pillars and has a silver disk beneath it, marking the exact place where the cross stood. The rock of Gologotha can be seen through a cavity in the center. On either side of the altar are black discs marking the site of the crosses of the two thieves crucified with Jesus. To the right of the altar is a fissure in the rock believed to have been caused by an earthquake at the time of the death of Jesus: *"and the earth did quake and the rocks rent...Now when the centurion and they that were with him, watching Jesus, saw the earthquake, and those things that were done, they feared greatly, saying, Truly this was the Son of God".* (Matthew 28:51,54)

The Stone of Anointing (Unction)

An archaeological find giving unique historical evidence about death by crucifixion in time of Christ. The ankles of the crucified man are pierced with an iron nail.

13th Station
Jesus is taken down from the Cross

The Stone of Anointing - An altar marks the spot where Mary received the body of Jesus after He had been taken down from the Cross. Jesus' body was then laid out on the Stone of Unction (Anointing) and anointed with a mixture of myrrh, aloe and aromatic oils in preparation for burial.

Crusader marble statue
from the Church
of the Holy Sepulcher
◄ ....

The Holy Sepulcher

14th Station
Jesus is placed in the Tomb

The Holy Sepulcher, the holiest place in Christendom, lies in the center of the Rotunda in a richly decorated edicule. The tomb was originally in a cave hewn in the rock, and the Rotunda was built over and around it. The sacred rock is covered with marble and above it are paintings depicting the Resurrection. The tomb itself is covered by a smooth marble slab, which has been in place since 1555. Over the tomb, 42 lamps - thirteen each for the Latins, Greek Orthodox and Armenians and four for the Copts - burn day and night.

"And when Joseph had taken the body, he wrapped it in a clean linen cloth, and laid it in his own new tomb which he had hewn out in the rock"   (Matthew 27:59-60)

The first room inside the Sepulcher is the Chapel of the Angel. Here, Mary Magdalene, visiting the grave and finding the body gone on the first Sunday after the Crucifixion, saw an angel in white sitting on a stone altar. The pilaster in the center of the room contains a piece of the stone with which the sepulcher was closed.

"And they saw a young man sitting on the right side, clothed in a long white garment: and they were affrighted".

(Mark 16:5)

The Chapel of the Angel

The Chapel of St. Helena

This graffiti carved on bedrock beneath the Church of the Holy Sepulcher depicts a ship with a broken mast, and the Latin words "Domine Ivimus", "Lord, we shall go up". It may have been carved in thanksgiving for a safe arrival in Jerusalem by very early Christian pilgrims.

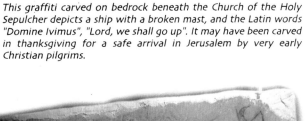

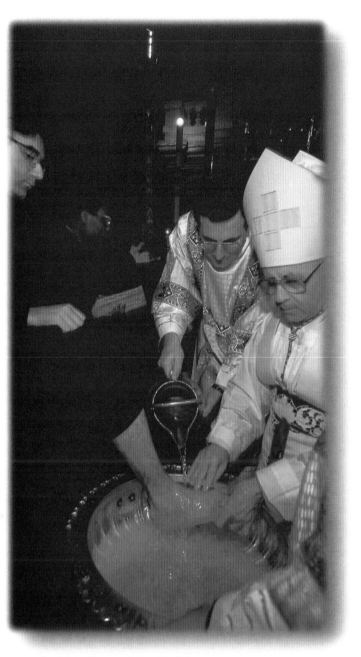

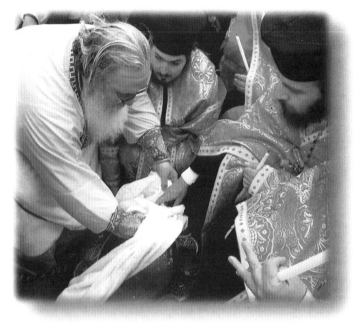

> "*Now in this place where He was crucified there was a garden; and in a garden a new sepulchre wherein was never man yet laid.*"
>
> (John 19:41)

Many Protestants believe that Jesus is buried in the Garden Tomb, which is set in a quiet enclosure just outside Damascus Gate. A nearby hillock, with a Moslem cemetery on top and a broken cistern in its rocky face, bears resemblance to a skull which could be Gologotha. In 1867, a first-century rock-hewn tomb containing two chambers was discovered near the hill. In 1882, the British General Gordon was a leading advocate for this area as a probable site of the Crucifixion and it was purchased by the Garden Tomb Association of London in 1893. The evidence for a probable site of execution near to an exceptionally large cistern and a Herodian tomb, which meets all the details mentioned in the Gospels, makes the present garden a center for Christian meditation.

The Garden Tomb

Emmaus

"And behold, two of them went that day to a village called Emmaus, which was from Jerusalem about three-score furlongs" (Luke 24:13)

The exact location of the site of Emmaus is not known. It is believed to be the little settlement located about 16 kilometers west of Jerusalem.

The Church of Emmaus (El Qubeibeh)

The Church of Emmaus
(El Qubeibeh)

At Emmaus, Jesus met Cleophas and Simon after His Resurrection and ate with them. The Franciscans built a church on the spot where Cleophas' house was believed to have stood. Others believe that the site of Emmaus is where the Trappist Monastery at Latrun now stands.

A painting in the Church at Emmaus ,
depicting Jesus breaking bread
while eating with Cleophas and a companion.

The stained glass windows
of the Franciscan Basilica at Emmaus

1 - *"That very day two of them were going to a village named Emmaus".*   (Luke 24:13)

2 - *"While they were talking and discussing together. Jesus himself drew near and went with them. But their eyes kept from recognizing him".*   (Luke 24:15-16)

3 - *"When he was at table with them, he took the bread and blessed, and broke it and gave it to them. And their eyes were opened and they recognized him".*

(Luke 24:30-31)

4 - *"And they rose that same hour and returned to Jerusalem ; and they found the eleven gathered together... Then they told what had happened on the road, and how he was know to them in the breaking of the bread".*

(Luke 24:33-35)

Jesus meets the disciples on the road to Emmaus.   *The two disciples of Jesus on the road to Emmaus.*   *Jesus at table with the two disciples at Emmaus.*   *The two disciples of Emmaus back in Jerusalem with eleven.*

The Dome of the Rock

The Dome of the Rock was built by the Moslem Caliph Abd El Malik on the site of the First and Second Temples in 691. Moslems believe that this is the site of Mohammed's ascent to heaven on his winged steed. The octagonal structure is similar in form and artistic design to St. Peter's house in Capernaum, and its Byzantine-style decorations were executed by the many Byzantine artists still living in the city at the time of its construction. It has four doors, and eight marble pillars and sixteen columns support the wooden ceiling which is richly decorated with stucco painted in red and gold. A silver candelabra once hung from the center; all that remains now is the great chain. The mosaic decorations and arches are all from the original construction, as are the inscriptions from the Koran in the cupola. The stained-glass windows are from renovations made by Suleiman the Magnificent, who also replaced the original mosaics with tiles. The roof was gold-plated in 1994.

In the center of the Dome of the Rock is the rock of Mount Moriah on which, according to Jewish tradition, Abraham was about to sacrifice Isaac, while Moslems believe that it was Ishmael. Here stood the Ark of the Covenant in the First Temple.

◄......................
Washing feet before entering the Mosque

View of the interior of the Dome of the Rock through a fish-eye lens.

The Dome of the Rock

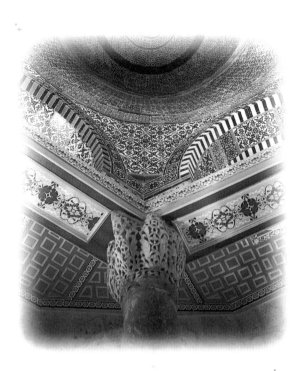

Detail of the decorations
on the inside
of the Dome of the Rock

Detail of the decorations
at the Dome of the Rock

One of the five windows
in the Dome of the Rock

Detail
of the decorations
on the outside
of the Dome
of the Rock

Solomon's Stables are subterranean vaults where the Crusaders kept their horses.

Interior of the Mosque of El Aksa

The Mosque of El Aksa

Jerusalem's main mosque is the silver-domed El Aksa, "the furthest". The original mosque was constructed in the early eighth century by Caliph Walid, son of Abd El Malik. Prone to frequent earthquakes, the mosque has often been rebuilt so that there are only few remains of the original building. The roof rests on beautifully decorated pillars and arches and the floor is covered with priceless rugs. From 1099-1187, the Crusaders used the mosque as headquarters of the Templar knights, but after the defeat of the Crusaders, Saladdin restored it as a mosque.

The Walls of the Old City

The city walls, constructed of great blocks of stone, are basically those built by the Turkish sultan Suleiman between 1539 and 1542 on the foundations of the Roman Aelia Capitolina. They measure 2 1/2 miles in circumference and vary in height according to the conformation of the land.

"Our feet shall stand within thy gates, O Jerusalem".   (Psalm 122:2)

The Golden Gate

The seventh century Golden Gate is situated on the site of the original eastern gate of the Temple compound. According to Christian tradition, Jesus passed through this gate, which is opposite the Mount of Olives, when entering Jerusalem with His disciples on Palm Sunday. The gate has been walled up since the ninth century. According to Jewish tradition, the Messiah will enter Jerusalem through this gate. However, since he will be a member of the priesthood who may not go into a cemetery, the Moslems built a cemetery here to prevent his coming. This cemetery is still in use.

Damascus Gate

The Damascus Gate in the northern wall was built by Suleiman the Magnificent over the remains of previous gates. The original site was a Herodian structure, followed in 135 A.D by an entrance into Hadrian's Aelia Capitolina. The Damascus Gate is one of the most impressive and decorative gates in the walls of the Old City.

The column of Damascus Gate in the Medaba map

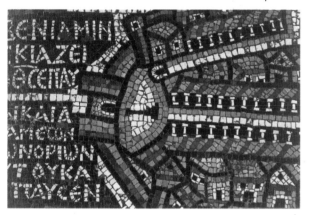

Damascus Gate at night

The gate from the Roman period

The New Gate
Dung Gate

Zion Gate

Herod's Gate

St. Stephen's Gate (also called Lion's Gate)

Jaffa Gate

Below: The Citadel adjoining Jaffa Gate was once the fortress that guarded Herod's Palace; it is one of the most well-known landmarks of Jerusalem. Today the Museum of the City of Jerusalem is located inside the Citadel and other changing exhibitions are held frequently. A summer attraction is the "Sound and Light" show telling the story of the Citadel throughout its history.

The "Tower of David", Herod's Citadel

The Citadel was built by Herod. Within it were three towers which he called after the people he loved - Mariamne, his wife, Phasael, his brother and Hippicus, his friend. Of these three towers only the bottom half of one tower remained after the destruction of the city by the Romans. In the last few years, excavations have unearthed remains from as far back as the Hasmonean period. The minaret tower from a later period is erroneously known as the "Tower of David". It was used as a Moslem prayer house and is called by the Arabs "David's Prayer Cell", as Moslems believe that David prayed here.

Restored arch of the Hurva Synagogue

The Western Wall Tunnels

Only part of Herod's retaining Western Wall is visible at ground level. The rest is underground and was excavated by the British archaeologists Wilson and Warren. Excavations have uncovered remains from the time of King Solomon. Today one can walk along the ancient Herodian street, along which Jesus may have walked, at a depth of 50 feet below ground level, the length of the wall. The tunnel passes stairs from the time of the Second Temple, through the remains of Wilson's Arch where a road to the Temple passed in Herodian times, a Hasmonean water tunnel, a pool and an ancient quarry.

Medieval street built over the remains of the ancient bridge connecting the city to the Temple Mount

Prayers at the Western Wall on weekdays and festivals

The Western Wall

Ever since the destruction of the Second Temple in 70 A.D., Jews have gathered in pilgrimage and prayer at the Western Wall, which has become known as the Wailing Wall. Its cracks are filled with hastily written prayers for the speedy recovery of the sick, for the peace of Jerusalem and the coming of the Messiah.

Interior of the Shrine of the Book

The Shrine of the Book

The Shrine of the Book

The Shrine of the Book at the Israel Museum contains the priceless biblical scrolls and scroll fragments found at Qumran. The building was especially designed to symbolize their discovery. Its dome is in the shape of the cover of the jars within which the scrolls were found. The black basalt wall symbolizes the Sons of Darkness whilst the Shrine itself is a sparkling white for the Sons of Light, which is generally considered a reference to the Essenes. Within the Shrine, a central display case represents the wooden roller of a Torah Scroll. The Bar Kochba letters, various relics and household effects found at the site of the discovery are displayed in niches in the long tunnel-like entrance of the Shrine of the Book.

A portion of the Isaiah Scroll

The Model of Ancient Jerusalem in the grounds of the Israel Museum

The Antonia Fortress

Professor Avi-Yonah of the Hebrew University put many years of research and work into producing this 1:50 scale model of the City of Jerusalem at the time of the Second Temple, the time of Jesus. It is constructed mainly from the original materials used in the buildings it represents - marble, stone, copper and wood, according to measurements given in Middot in the Mishnah, and also to fit the descriptions in the books of Josephus Flavius. The splendid Second Temple dominated the scene of Jerusalem's magnificence and beauty in 66 A.D and Herod's Palace, the twin-spired Palace of the Hasmoneans, the Roman theater, the markets, inns and common dwelling places are all easily identifiable. When excavations reveal new information, changes are made in the model.

The hill of Golgotha

The Temple

Hebron

Hebron is one of the world's oldest cities. Genesis 23 relates how *"Sarah died in Kirjath Arba; the same is Hebron"*, and *"Abraham buried Sarah his wife in the cave of Machpelah before Mamre: the same is Hebron"*, in the field which he bought from Ephron the Hittite for four hundred shekels of silver. Abraham himself was later buried here as were Isaac, Rebecca, Jacob and Leah. Herod the Great erected the wall encircling the compound and paved the enclosure. In Byzantine times it was roofed over and turned into the Church of Abraham, but with the Moslem invasion of 638 it became the Mosque of Abraham and has remained so ever since apart from the period of the Crusaders.

Symbolic cenotaphs set over the graves in the mausoleum of the Patriarchs and Matriarchs.

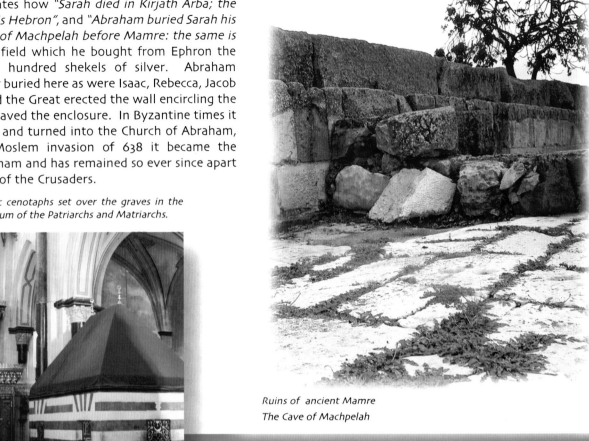

Ruins of ancient Mamre
The Cave of Machpelah

The Bedouin

The nomadic lifestyle of the Bedouin is reminiscent of Biblical times and the laws governing their society are similar to the laws of Moses, whom they revere. The Bedouin are divided into tribes, each with a chief, the Sheikh, elected by adult males to oversee their tribal interests. Bedouin hospitality is well known - in winter, guests are welcomed to a tent of woven goats' hair, while in summer they are protected from the hot rays of the sun by a thatched shelter. Raising livestock, especially camels, sheep and goats which also provide milk, cheese, hair and skins, is the traditional occupation of these people. However, times and habits are changing. Bedouin dwellings are now often huts or houses instead of tents, and automobiles are ousting the camel. Many men work in the tourist or building industries while the women work at home on Bedouin arts and crafts to sell to tourists. Strangers are never asked questions and will immediately be offered refreshments, while honored guests will be served with meat of a precious goat from the herd, specially slaughtered for them.

Megiddo - Armageddon

Due to its strategic position on the Via Maris, Megiddo was a major battleground in the past. Excavations have revealed the remains of twenty superimposed cities on this site, the oldest dating back to 4000 B.C. An underground water tunnel linked the inhabitants to the water source located beyond the walls and a Canaanite temple, palaces, storehouses, sentry towers and solders' quarters were all contained within the wall. According to tradition, this is the site of Armageddon where the final battle between the forces of good and evil will take place.

The water tunnel

Canaanite altar at Megiddo

Samaria

Jacob's Well, Nablus

The Well of Jacob was dug by the Patriarch over 3000 years ago. John 4 tells how Jesus, on his way to the Galilee, came *"to a city of Samaria...now Jacob's well was there"*. He sat down by the well that Jacob had given to his son Joseph when a Samaritan woman came to draw water and Jesus said to her: *"Give me to drink"*. The well is in the crypt of the church built by Helena, mother of Emperor Constantine. The first church was destroyed and a second one, rebuilt by the Crusaders, was also destroyed.

Nearby Shechem, today Nablus, was an important city at the time of the Patriarchs and later during the period of the Judges. However, it declined when the kings of Israel moved their palace to Samaria. It was overrun by the Assyrians in 721 B.C and later rebuilt by Alexander the Great as a Greek town and again by King Herod, who changed its name to Sebaste. Under Roman rule it continued to be a magnificent city but later fell into obscurity. There are impressive Greek, Herodian and Roman remains which have been partially restored.

Ruins of the Roman forum - Sebaste (Samaria)

Bet Shean

et Shean, the Greek Scythopolis, was one of the great cities of olden times. During the time of Jesus, it was one of the Graeco-Roman cities of the Decapolis, an alliance of cities on both sides of the Jordan. Excavations have revealed signs of habitation from 4000 B.C. There are impressive remains from the Roman and Byzantine periods including a partially restored theater, some public buildings with mosaics and a colonnaded street which was once lined with shops.

Belvoir and the Jordan Valley in the background

◄ ....

*"Tyche" fragment
of the mosaic floor
of a Byzantine
public building*

The Roman Theater

Tiberias

Tiberias, the capital of the Galilee, is situated 209 meters below sea-level on the south-west shore of the Sea of Galilee. It was founded around 20 A.D by Herod Antipas, son of Herod the Great. Although Tiberias was situated within the radius of Jesus' ministry, Christianity did not make much headway here until the late Byzantine period. Conquered by the Arabs in 636, then by the Crusaders who remained in power from 1100 to 1247, it was utilized by both as an administrative center. Many of the stories from the Gospel took place around this area of Galilee.

South of Tiberias is Hamat, its hot mineral springs making it into a spa as popular today as it was with Roman officials and their families 2000 years ago.

Mosaic floor of the ancient Hamat synagogue

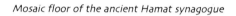

The Greek Orthodox Monastery at Tiberias
Bird's eye view of Tiberias

The church on the hill of Bereniki, Tiberias

Mount Arbel

Mount Arbel is referred to in Hosea 10:14 as the "battlefield of Beit-arbel". Herod launched an all-out campaign against the Zealots who had entrenched themselves in the caves, and Josephus tells a tragic story of a father who killed his seven children, his wife and himself rather than be taken captive. There are remains of a third century synagogue at the site.

The Horns of Hittin

It was at the double-peaked Horns of Hittin where the Crusaders met a decisive defeat at the hands of Saladin in 1187, resulting in the end of the Latin Kingdom of Jerusalem. Some parts of the Holy Land were later restored to Christian control during the Third Crusade, but the glorious days of the Crusaders were never restored.

Mount Arbel with the Sea of Galilee ▶

Mount Arbel and the Sea of Galilee seen from the Horns of Hittin

The "Tachanah" waterfall near Metulla

Tel Hazor, with Kibbutz Ayelet Hashahar in the background

The Hula Valley

At the end of the nineteenth century, when Jewish pioneers came to settle the Hula Valley on land purchased by Baron Rothschild, the land was inundated with swamps plagued by malarial mosquitoes which caused many deaths. In the 1950's, 12,000 acres of land was drained and transformed into fertile fields. The Hula Nature Reserve is the last remnant of these swamps, once teeming with water buffalo and wild boar, turtles and other water creatures, rare fish and wading birds leading a primeval existence among the aquatic plants and creepers.

Mount Hermon

The huge Mount Hermon, lying partly in Lebanon and Syria, towers above the Golan Heights and mountains of the Upper Galilee. At an altitude of 2814 meters, the rain and snow it receives are the most important factors influencing the water system of the region. Psalm 133 says *"how good and how pleasant it is for brethren to dwell together in unity! It is ...as the dew of Hermon"* while Psalm 89 says *"Tabor and Hermon shall rejoice in thy name"*.

Mount Hermon and the Hula Valley

Acre

Acre, also known as Ptolemais, was an important city and harbor from ancient times. *"And when we had finished our course from Tyre we came to Ptolemais, and saluted the brethren, and abode with them one day" (Acts 21:7).*

Its heyday was during the time of the Crusaders. In 1104, they made it their capital, setting up the Kingdom of Acre which was ruled by the Knights of St. John and lasted until 1291. During this period, Acre's wealth and economic output were legendary. The wonderfully preserved, now subterranean, Crusaders' city with its enormous complex of knights' halls with vaulted ceilings bear witness to its greatness. These halls were used as living quarters, dining halls, a hospice and for ceremonial purposes. A secret underground tunnel led to the harbor to enable the knights to flee in case of siege. In 1775, Ahmed el-Jazzar, known as "the Butcher" for his cruelty, erected the Great Mosque, using marble columns shipped in from Ashkelon and Caesarea. With the help of the British, el-Jazzar staved off Napolean's two-month siege of Acre in 1799. After the advent of steamships, the port lost its importance.

The Mosque of El-Jazzar
St. John's Crypt.

The Marina

Haifa

The Bahai Shrine

The city of Haifa is built above the harbor on the slopes of Mount Carmel and its landscape is dominated by the golden dome of the Bahai Temple. Set in the formal Persian gardens is the grave of the Persian-born Bab - the Gate, or the Forerunner - who was executed in 1850 at the age of 31 for his religious teachings. The Bahai faith stresses the Unity of God and the Brotherhood of Mankind.

Haifa is a modern harbor able to accommodate all sorts of luxury liners, tankers, cargo boats and other ships. It is also one of Israel's main centers of high technology, fostered by the Technion and Haifa University which turn out highly-qualified engineers and scholars in every field. Ideally situated between the sea and the forested Mount Carmel, of which Isaiah 35:2 says *"the excellency of Carmel"*, the environs of haifa have been a favorite habitation for untold generations. Prehistoric man lived here in the caves of Carmel and, before the coming of the Israelites, there were Phoenicians at Shikmona on the coast who introduced the art of glass-making with the fine silica sand on the shore.

Bird's eye view of Haifa

Stella Maris

The largest Carmelite Monastery and world center of the Order stands at the top of the promontory with a magnificent view of the city of Haifa. It is built on the site of earlier churches and monasteries of the Byzantine periods. The church was built over a cave associated with the prophets Elijah and Elisha. Nearby is the lighthouse called Stella Maris - Star of the Sea. In the lower garden of the monastery is the Cave of Elijah where, according to Christian tradition, the prophet lived.

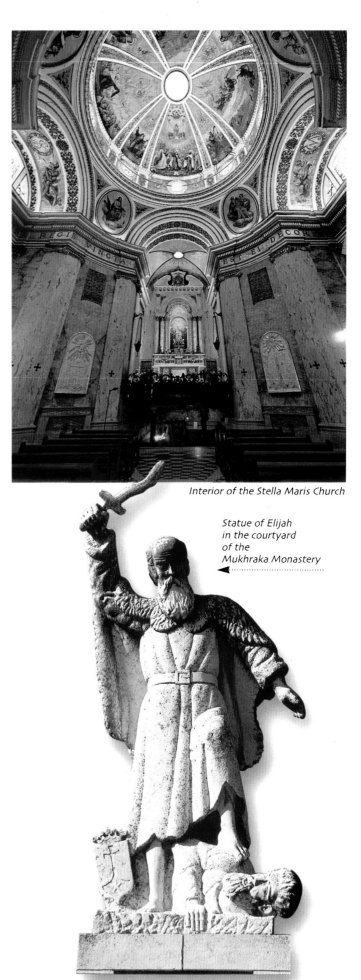

Interior of the Stella Maris Church

Shrine to Elijah in the Stella Maris Church

Mukhraka

The Canaanite inhabitants of the land worshipped Baal and his consort Ishtar, who were adopted by the Israelites. The prophet Elijah challenged the priests of Baal to prove whose god was more powerful and when he won, the Israelites abandoned the Canaanite deities and the false prophets were slaughtered (I Kings 18). Mukhraka, the traditional site of the contest, is marked by a Carmelite monastery, built in 1886.

Statue of Elijah in the courtyard of the Mukhraka Monastery

The Mukhraka

Caesarea

Part of a newly excavated mosaic

Roman marble statue re-erected in the Byzantine street.

The city of Caesarea was built by Herod the Great in 20 B.C and named after Caesar Augustus. It was one of the most splendid cities of the ancient world, supplied with all the luxuries that made up Graeco-Roman culture - an amphitheater, theater, a hippodrome and hot baths. For 600 years, it was the capital of the Roman province of Judea and official residence of its governors, including Pontius Pilate. Simon Peter preached to a gentile congregation here at the house of Cornelius the Centurion and from here Paul was sent to Tarsus. Here in 66 A.D began the Jewish revolt against the Romans which was to culminate in the destruction of Jerusalem and the Temple. The Crusaders rebuilt Caesarea as a citadel-town and the massive fortified walls and moat from this period still remain.

Bird's eye view of Caesarea

Jaffa

From time immemorial, Jaffa has been important as a port and station on the ancient trade route, the Via Maris, which connected Egypt with Mesopotamia and the north. Jaffa is the biblical port-town of Joppa which, according to legend, was founded by Noah's son Japhet. Solomon had wood from the Lebanon floated by sea to Jaffa for building the Temple in Jerusalem. The story of Jonah and the whale is associated with Jaffa, for Jonah set sail from here on his journey to Nineveh. Here Peter restored Tabitha to life and *"tarried for many days with one Simon the Tanner"* (Acts 9:43). Here he had his vision which led to the first preaching of the gospel of Christ to the Gentiles. The House of Simon the Tanner and St. Peter's Church recall these events.

In 1909, a number of Jews wanted to escape the cramped quarters of Jaffa and founded Tel Aviv in the sand-dunes north of the city. Today, Tel Aviv is a modern metropolis, Israel's most cosmopolitan city and center of culture and entertainment.

Old Jaffa

View of Tel Aviv from Old Jaffa

Ashdod

Ashdod was one of the five major Philistine cities together with Ashkelon, Ekron, Gath and Gaza which were interwoven with the actions of the Israelites as recorded in the book of Judges, and particularly with the wanderings of the Ark. *"The Philistines took the ark of God and brought it from Ebenezer unto Ashdod... and there they brought it into the house of Dagon"* (I Samuel 5) with disastrous consequences. Ashdod is the New Testament Azotus, and today is a large port.

Ashdod Yam,
ancient Ashdod
◄ ·······················

Part of a Roman sarcophagus

Ashkelon

Ashkelon was, 4000 years ago, a Canaanite city-state under Egyptian protection. Later, it became one of the five major Philistine cities. Under Greek domination, it was an independent city and traditionally the birthplace of Herod the Great. When he came to power, he built palatial buildings and colonnaded walks here, adding statues and fountains. Ashkelon flourished during Roman and Byzantine times and later became one of the key coastal fortresses of the Crusaders. After their defeat it lay neglected for centuries and today is a residential and vacation town.

Many of the columns, capitals and statues of ancient Ashkelon have been placed in the National Park.

Ancient wine jars
found in Ashkelon
◄ ·······················

Ancient relief
in the
National Park
······················· ►

Roman Statue:
Mother and Child

At the Bedouin market

Abraham's Well

Beersheba

Beersheba, the capital of the Negev, is associated with Abraham and the Patriarchs. Abraham and Abimelech *"made a covenant at Beer-sheba... and Abraham planted a grove in Beer-sheba"* (Genesis 21:32-33). From here he sent away his Egyptian handmaid Hagar and their son Ishmael, and here God called on him to sacrifice his son Isaac. Later it became the southernmost point of settlement, for Judges 20:1 describes how the *"children of Israel went out, and the congregation was gathered together as one man from Dan even to Beer-sheba"*. Excavations have revealed cave dwellings from 4000 B.C and a complete town from the time of the Judges. Every Thursday morning a Bedouin market is held here.

Bird's eye view of Beer Sheba

The Nabateans

The Nabateans were a trading nation who had their beginnings around the third century B.C and over the years grew in power and importance by controlling the caravan routes. These routes linked Gaza on the Mediterranean to Eilat on the Red Sea, extended across to Arabia, transporting perfumes and spices, and up through Jerusalem to the lands of the north. Their capital was Petra, now in Jordan, and their heyday was between the second century B.C and the first century A.D., when the Romans changed their status from that of an empire into a Roman province. There were five Nabatean towns in the Negev, known together as the Pentapolis: Avdat, Shivta, Mamshit, Kalutza and Nitzana, the first three of which have been restored. The Nabatean system of water collection and storage was remarkable, making the desert blossom and since the 1950's, experiments have been made to copy their methods. Inscriptions found on Nabatean sites are in Aramaic, a language similar to Hebrew.

An ancient
wine-press
in Avdat

Remains
of an
ancient church
at Avdat

Eilat

Eilat is Israel's southernmost town, situated at the head of the Gulf of Eilat, opening into the Red Sea. It was first mentioned in Numbers 33:35. At first, life in Eilat was quiet, until communications improved and it became an integral part of the rest of the country. Tourists began to flock to Eilat to enjoy the incredible all-year-round sunshine and summer temperatures, the sea, water-sports, hotels and nightlife. Today it is a popular holiday resort and a base for touring the sights and wonders of the desert. Among these are the Timna copper mines which have produced copper on and off for 6000 years. Unproven tales associate the Timna mines with King Solomon.

Partial view of Eilat

Eilat, underwater scenery in the Red Sea

King Solomon's Pillars

Untamed beauty of the surrounding desert

The Medaba Map

Medaba is an ancient city in Transjordan which is mentioned in Numbers 21:30. Christians lived in this large settlement during the Roman and Byzantine period, building houses and churches.

When a Greek Orthodox Church was erected in 1884 on the ruins of an earlier church from the sixth century A.D., the mosaic map was discovered. It portrays the Holy Land and its neighbours.

The Greek name-places are those of settlements mentioned in the Bible.

The following is a list of some of the places and incidents shown on the map:

1. **The Dead Sea.**
1A. **Adam and Eve with the serpent**.
   The mosaic was disfigured, in keeping with the custom of the times not to portray human figures.
2. **The hot baths.**
3. **The Jordan River flowing into the Dead Sea.**
4. **Jericho** - one of the oldest cities in the world. An oasis, where date palms, sub-tropical fruits and exotic flowers grow in abundance.
5. **The Mountains of Moab.**
6. **Jerusalem** - the map depicts the two main roads with avenues of columns. Parts of one of these avenues - the Cardo - have been excavated and reconstructed. The mosaic also shows the Tower of David, the Church of the Holy Sepulcher, Mount Zion, the Damascus Gate and the Pillar of Hadrian.
7. **Bethlehem.**
8. **Judah.**
9. **Hebron - the Cave of Machpelah.**
10. **Tekoah.**
11. **Emmaus.**
12. **Lydda** (Lod)
13. **Yavneh** - on the coast, where the Sanhedrin was re-established by Jews who had managed to escape from Jerusalem, when it was razed by Titus in 70 A.D.
14. **The Tribe of Dan.**
15. **Jaffa-** the sanctuary of Jonah the Prophet.
16. **Jacob's Well - Nablus**. Dug by the Patriarch over 3,000 years ago.
   This is considered a hallowed spot and has remained a place of pilgrimage over the centuries.

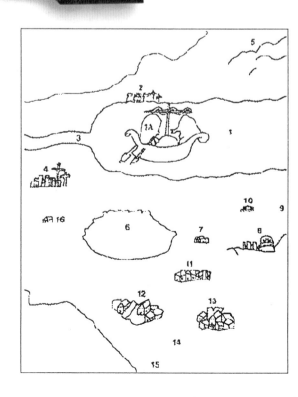